Fly Fishing
IN IDAHO

PHOTOGRAPHY BY R. RANDOLPH ASHTON
TEXT BY WILL GODFREY
INTRODUCTION BY TERRY RING

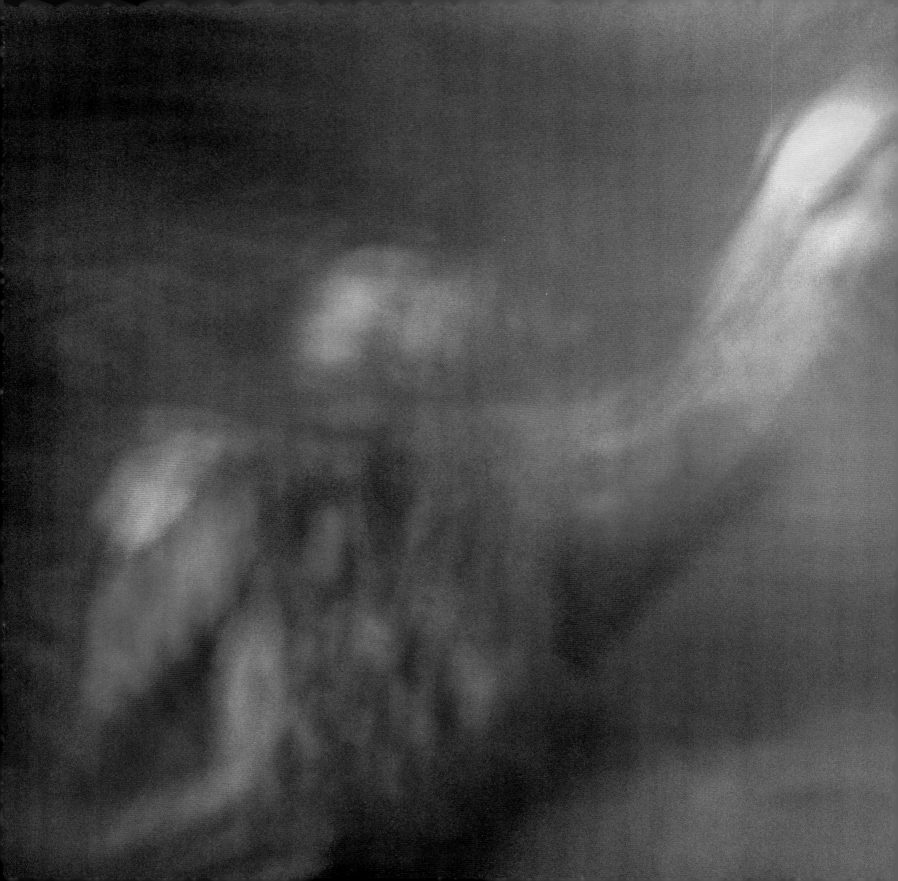

I WOULD LIKE TO DEDICATE THIS BOOK TO MY MOTHER FOR KEEPING MY HEART FILLED WITH LOVE AND TO MY FATHER FOR ALWAYS SHOWING ME WHERE THE RIVERS RUN.

-R. RANDOLPH ASHTON
WINTER 2006

BIG LOST RIVER
TIM BOHLIN®

Fly Fishing IN IDAHO

PHOTOGRAPHY	R. RANDOLPH ASHTON
TEXT	WILL GODFREY
EDITOR	CARRIE LIGHTNER
CREATIVE DIRECTOR	DAVID R. STOECKLEIN
ART DIRECTION & DESIGN	SARAH SNYDER
IMAGE SCANNING AND RETOUCHING	SARAH SNYDER, MARK OLIVER

COVER PHOTO - MESA FALLS OF THE HENRY'S FORK, DILLON WITMER
BACK COVER PHOTO - BAMBOO FLY ROD

All images in this book are available as signed original gallery prints and for stock photography usage.

Other books by Stoecklein Publishing include *The Cowboy Hat, The American Quarter Horse, Cattle, The Cowboy Boot, Outhouses, Western Fences, Saddles of the West, California Missions, Dude Ranches of the American West, The Spur, The Western Buckle, Ranch Style, Cowgirls in Heaven, The Performance Horse, Cow Dogs, Lil' Buckaroos, The American Paint Horse, The Idaho Cowboy, Cowboy Gear, Don't Fence Me In, The Texas Cowboys, The Montana Cowboy, The Western Horse, Cowgirls, Spirit of the West*, and *The California Cowboy*.

Stoecklein Photography & Publishing
1730 Lear Lane, Unit A
Hailey, Idaho 83333
tel 208.788.4593 fax 208.788.4713 toll-free 800.727.5191
WWW.THESTOECKLEINCOLLECTION.COM

Printed in China
Copyright © 2006 Stoecklein Publishing
Photography Copyright © R. Randolph Ashton

ISBN-10: 1-933192-63-1
ISBN-13: 978-193319263-5
Library of Congress Catalog number 2005937518

PUBLISHER'S NOTE

It gives me great pride to introduce you all to Randy Ashton, a young and very talented photographer. This book is one that I always wanted to photograph myself, but I just can't do it all. It has taken me many years to learn that, and I really enjoyed editing this book for Randy. Frankly, I was envious that I had not taken these photographs myself; they have inspired me in my own work.

Idaho is my home state; this is where I live with my family. It is where Stoecklein Publishing began and has its roots. So we wanted the first fly fishing book that we published to feature the state we love so much. There are also fly fishing books in the works for Montana, Wyoming, Oregon, and Colorado. My ultimate dream is to cover all the great fly fishing states.

Fly fishing is a big part of the West and Stoecklein Publishing has always stood for the preservation of the West.

Fly fishermen understand the importance of clean mountain water — they understand the importance of the water to the fish and ultimately to all of us.

For many fly fishermen, fly fishing is spiritual...water is life.

David R Stoecklein

BROWN TROUT

FOREWORD

WHAT I THOUGHT WAS JUST ANOTHER ROUTINE MEETING WITH MY BOSS, PHOTOGRAPHER DAVE STOECKLEIN, ACTUALLY TURNED INTO AN AMAZING OPPORTUNITY FOR ME. DAVE ASKED ME TO DO A PHOTOGRAPHY BOOK ON IDAHO FLY FISHING. THIS WAS AN OPPORTUNITY I HAD BEEN DREAMING ABOUT SINCE THE DAY I PICKED UP A CAMERA. AFTER DAVE FINISHED TALKING, I FLEW OUT THE DOOR BEFORE HE COULD CHANGE HIS MIND AND SET OUT ON THE CHANCE OF A LIFETIME.

I STARTED OUT BY CALLING OUTFITTERS AND RANCHERS AND MAPPING OUT TRIPS TO RIVERS THROUGHOUT IDAHO. I HAVE BEEN AN AVID FLY FISHERMAN ALMOST SINCE BIRTH AND WAS WELL ACQUAINTED WITH SILVER CREEK, BIG WOOD RIVER, AND HENRY'S FORK, MY FAVORITE SPOTS TO FISH WITH MY FATHER WHEN I WAS YOUNG. I HAD ALSO FISHED THE CLEARWATER IN NORTHERN IDAHO FOR STEELHEAD TROUT. BUT THAT WAS PRETTY MUCH THE EXTENT OF MY KNOWLEDGE OF FLY FISHING IN THE GEM STATE. AS A RESIDENT OF KETCHUM, I AM FORTUNATE TO KNOW MANY OF THE GUIDES AT SILVER CREEK OUTFITTERS. THEY PROVIDED ME WITH INVALUABLE INFORMATION ABOUT OTHER GREAT FLY FISHING SPOTS IN IDAHO. MOST OF THE OUTFITTERS I CALLED IN OTHER PARTS OF THE STATE WERE ALSO EXTREMELY HELPFUL AND ENCOURAGING.

DURING MY TRAVELS, I WAS NOT PREPARED FOR THE GRANDEUR THAT IDAHO OFFERS ITS FISHERMEN. WHILE LIVING IN A TENT FOR A YEAR, I CAME ACROSS TROUT-INFESTED RIVERS, MOUNTAINS BEGGING TO BE HIKED, CRYSTAL CLEAR LAKES, AND SOME OF THE NICEST PEOPLE ON EARTH.

IDAHO IS BLESSED WITH TWO OF THE WORLD'S MOST FAMOUS SPRING CREEKS, SILVER CREEK AND HENRY'S FORK ON THE SNAKE RIVER. THESE TWO RIVERS ALONE PLACE IDAHO AMONG THE TOP FLY FISHING DESTINATIONS IN THE UNITED STATES. BUT SILVER CREEK AND HENRY'S FORK ARE JUST THE BEGINNING. THERE ARE LESSER KNOWN BUT EQUALLY PRODUCTIVE SPRING CREEKS THROUGHOUT THE STATE—TAIL WATERS WITH CONSISTENT WATER TEMPERATURES PERFECT FOR TROUT (SUCH AS THE SOUTH FORK OF THE BOISE RIVER), FREESTONE RIVERS LARGE AND SMALL, TINY MOUNTAIN STREAMS FILLED WITH NATIVE CUTTHROATS AND BROOKIES, AND LAKES WHERE RAINBOWS AND BROWN TROUT ABOUND AND GROW LARGE. THERE ARE ALSO WONDERFUL STEELHEAD RUNS IN THE SNAKE RIVER AND ITS TRIBUTARIES IN WESTERN IDAHO AND HUGE BULL TROUT INHABITING MANY OF THE STREAMS OF NORTHERN IDAHO. ONE CAN EVEN FIND GOLDEN TROUT, GRAYLING, AND SEVERAL SPECIES OF SALMON IN IDAHO RIVERS AND STREAMS. FEW OTHER STATES CAN OFFER THIS KIND OF DIVERSITY FOR THE FRESHWATER ANGLER.

IDAHO'S RAW NATURAL BEAUTY MAKES IT A PERFECT SUBJECT FOR PHOTOGRAPHERS. MUCH OF NORTHERN AND CENTRAL IDAHO IS UNTAMED WILDERNESS, COMPLETELY UNSPOILED BY HUMANS. THE FRANK CHURCH RIVER OF NO RETURN WILDERNESS IS AN ENORMOUS EXPANSE OF CLEAR RIVERS, DEEP CANYONS, AND RUGGED MOUNTAINS. THE SAWTOOTH MOUNTAINS PROVIDE SOME OF THE MOST SPECTACULAR SCENERY IN THE WORLD. THE ONLY MOUNTAINS OF EQUAL GRANDEUR IN THE UNITED STATES ARE THE GRAND TETONS. AND, WHILE THEY ARE ACTUALLY ALONG THE IDAHO BORDER IN WYOMING, THEY DOMINATE THE HORIZON ALONG THE HENRY'S FORK, THE TETON RIVER, AND MANY OTHER TROUT STREAMS IN EASTERN IDAHO.

I HOPE I HAVE DONE JUSTICE TO THE FABULOUS FISHING SPOTS AND NATURAL BEAUTY OF IDAHO IN THIS BOOK. I HAVE TRIED TO DEPICT NOT ONLY THE BEAUTY OF THE STATE AND ITS RIVERS BUT ALSO THE PASSIONATE ANGLERS WHO WADE THESE RIVERS DURING THE FISHING SEASON. IN ANY EVENT, IT WAS AN INCREDIBLE EXPERIENCE TO TRAVEL THE ROADS AND RIVERS OF IDAHO, ENJOYING ITS REMARKABLE SCENERY AND MEETING THE PEOPLE WHO INHABIT AND VISIT THIS WONDERFUL STATE. PLEASE ENJOY THIS BOOK AND ALWAYS REMEMBER TO TREAT THE LAND WITH RESPECT AND RELEASE WHAT YOU CATCH.

TIGHT LINES,

R. RANDOLPH ASHTON

WALTER'S POND
BIG LOST RANGE
THREE SISTER'S RANCH

INTRODUCTION

SOME OF MY EARLIEST MEMORIES ARE RECOLLECTIONS OF TIME SPENT ON THE WATER, FISHING WITH MY FATHER. MY MOTHER SAYS THAT I WAS AN IMPATIENT AND ACTIVE CHILD, YET FISHING COULD HOLD MY INTEREST AND CAPTURE MY IMAGINATION FOR DAYS. GROWING UP IN COEUR D' ALENE, MY FATHER AND I FISHED THE LAKES, RIVERS, AND STREAMS OF THE IDAHO PANHANDLE. WE MOVED FROM NORTHERN TO SOUTHERN IDAHO WHEN I WAS IN HIGH SCHOOL AND I ACQUIRED A TASTE FOR IDAHO'S PREMIER DESERT FISHERIES WITH NAMES LIKE THE SOUTH FORK OF THE BOISE, SILVER CREEK, AND THE BIG LOST RIVER. MY COLLEGE YEARS TOOK ME TO THE EAST. GOING "EAST" IN IDAHO MEANS GOING TO THE HENRY'S FORK OF THE SNAKE RIVER WHERE I WORKED AS A FLY FISHING GUIDE FOR FIVE SEASONS.

I PURCHASED MY FIRST CAMERA WHEN I WAS A SOPHOMORE IN HIGH SCHOOL SO THAT I COULD TAKE SOME SNAPSHOTS OF A BACKPACKING TRIP TO IDAHO'S SAWTOOTH MOUNTAINS. I SHOT MY FIRST ROLL OF SLIDE FILM WHILE HIKING THE ALICE LAKE LOOP. THIS IS WHERE I FELL IN LOVE WITH THE MAGIC OF PHOTOGRAPHY.

I ENJOYED BOTH HOBBIES IMMENSELY EVEN THOUGH I LEARNED THAT FLY FISHERMEN AND PHOTOGRAPHERS SEE THE WORLD DIFFERENTLY. FLY FISHERMEN LOOK AT SNOW PACK, RIVER FLOW, WATER QUALITY, AND TEMPERATURE. INSECT HATCHES BECOME IMPORTANT. VACATIONS ARE PLANNED AROUND THESE HATCHES, LIKE THE GREEN DRAKE, THE SALMON FLY, AND THE TRICO. THESE HATCHES CAN OCCUR FOR FEW DAYS, A WEEK, OR MAYBE A MONTH, BUT THEY ONLY HAPPEN ONCE A YEAR. AN ANGLER LEARNS TO "READ THE WATER" LOOKING FOR CLUES TO WHERE THE FISH WILL BE HOLDING. NO TWO DAYS OF FISHING ARE EVER EXACTLY ALIKE AND AN ANGLER MUST ALWAYS BE AWARE OF THE FLUX AND CHANGE, AND EVEN PREDICT CHANGE THAT IS COMING.

ON THE OTHER HAND, A PHOTOGRAPHER IS ALWAYS LOOKING AT LIGHT, "READING THE SCENE" AND COMPOSING, INTERPRETING A THREE-DIMENSIONAL SPACE INTO A PICTURE. SOME IMAGES ARE PREDICTABLE, LIKE A BEAUTIFUL SCENIC SHOT, WHILE OTHERS REQUIRE BREAKING THE SCENE INTO SMALLER COMPONENTS, OR USING DEPTH OF FIELD TO ISOLATE A SUBJECT. NO TWO PHOTOGRAPHS ARE THE SAME. THE PHOTOGRAPHER'S WORLD IS A FROZEN MOMENT IN A UNIVERSE THAT IS CONSTANTLY CHANGING. THE PHOTOGRAPHER IS LESS CONCERNED WITH THE FUTURE THAN PRESERVING THE PAST.

WHILE GUIDING I ALWAYS CARRIED A CAMERA, TRYING TO CAPTURE THE FLEETING MOMENTS AS THEY PASSED BY. FISHING HAS TAKEN ME PLACES THAT I WOULD NOT HAVE OTHERWISE VISITED AND IT HAS SENT ME TO THESE PLACES WITH PEOPLE I WOULD NOT HAVE OTHERWISE MET, AND IT HAS SENT ME AT TIMES OF THE YEAR WHEN I WOULD NOT HAVE OTHERWISE BOTHERED. I AM GRATEFUL TO FLY FISHING FOR THESE GIFTS.

RANDY ASHTON WAS GIVEN MY DREAM ASSIGNMENT. HE HAS PHOTOGRAPHED THE FLY WATERS OF IDAHO WITH A PHOTOGRAPHER'S VISION. HIS BODY OF WORK EXTENDS FROM THE DESERT STREAMS OF SOUTHERN IDAHO TO THE FABULOUS HENRY'S FORK AREA OF EASTERN IDAHO AS WELL AS THE PANHANDLE, THE PLACE OF MY YOUTH. HE HAS MANAGED TO CAPTURE FLY FISHING IN THIS STATE FROM TOP TO BOTTOM, GIVING US SOMETHING TO CHERISH AND DREAM ABOUT, WHETHER WE ARE LOOKING DOWN A FLY ROD OR THROUGH A LENS.

TERRY RING
OWNER OF SILVER CREEK OUTFITTERS
KETCHUM, IDAHO

RAINBOW TROUT
BIG WOOD RIVER

Jay Ashton
Henry's Fork

A History of Fly Fishing in Idaho
by Will Godfrey

It has been said that at least one of the four rivers that ran east out of the Garden of Eden was really a river that ran out of Idaho. Perhaps the river was the Clearwater or the Henry's Fork. Maybe this river was the Salmon or Silver Creek. It may have been the Snake or perhaps the St. Joe. Is it possible that one of these great rivers ran east out of Eden? Well, maybe. Many believe that Idaho is the Eden of fly fishing, a proposition not too far removed from the truth now or in the past.

The great rivers of Idaho have been around for a long time—long before man used a fly rod to catch mighty cutthroat trout, grayling, and whitefish as well as sea runners, salmon, and steelhead native to the state. Fishing was a way of life for many but fishing with a fly in those early times was essentially non-existent. Fishing by hand, spear, and by net seemed to be the accepted ways. However, it is possible that the Nez Perce Indians were the first to fish with a "fly" in Idaho waters.

There is strong evidence that the Nez Perce had been fishing with what can only be described as 'sort of' fly-fishing techniques as long as 200 years ago. Elders relate how hooks were fashioned out of bone and wood and how feathers of grouse and other birds were attached with animal glue. Lines made from elk and deer sinew ensured that the catch could be (captured). When the Nez Perce acquired the horse in the early 1700s fishing lines were made from woven horsehair and small pieces of buckskin were used as bait. Balls of horsehair known as sniggles that would become entangled in the fishes' many teeth were also used to catch salmon and steelhead.[1]

Once the government purchased the Louisiana Territory in 1803, the area called Idaho became part of the United States as an undiscovered land. Long after Lewis and Clark, Osborne Russell, David Thompson, Andrew Henry, Donald McKenzie, and other noted "free trappers" had mapped, hunted, and fished the country, the 43rd state began to take shape. Two major interests helped to develop a widespread philosophy of independence and water resource use in those early days.

Mining interests in the north highlighted by Captain E.D. Pierce and the discovery of gold in Oro Fino Creek (Clark County) in 1860 brought a rush of miners into what was then part of the Washington Territory—Idaho today.

That same year and many miles to the south the community of Franklyn (Franklyn County) was established in southeast Idaho by agriculturally-based Mormon settlers from the Utah Territory and Salt Lake City. These two general movements helped establish people's attitudes toward the use of water and other wildlife. [2]

Wilford Woodruff, a Utah fisherman, had learned the skill of fly fishing while in England serving as a missionary for the Church of Jesus Christ of Latter-day Saints. He purchased a bamboo fly rod and single-action reel with some flies while he was there. In 1847 he brought these tools to the Utah area and recorded many of his fly fishing experiences in northern Utah and the Idaho Territories, which encompassed what we know as Franklyn, Bear Lake, and Caribou Counties of Idaho today.

Woodruff's journal recording from July 8, 1847 in the Fort Bridger area of Wyoming indicated that several other folks with him were also fishing, using fresh meat and grasshoppers with very little success. From all indications Wilford Woodruff was a better than average angler and he had the equipment to show off his fly fishing skills.

I went and flung my fly onto the water and it being the first time that I ever tried the artificial fly in America, or ever saw it tried, I watched as it floated upon the water with as much intense interest as Franklin did his kite when he tried to draw lightning from the skies. And as Franklin received great joy when he saw electricity or lighting descend on his kite string, in like manner was I highly gratified when I saw the nimble trout dart my fly, hook himself and run away with the line. I soon wearied him out and drew him to shore. I fished two or three hours including morning and evening and I caught twelve in all and about half of them would weigh about three-fourths of a pound each, while all the rest of the camp did not catch during the day three pounds of trout in all—proof positive to me that the artificial fly is far the best thing now known to fish trout with. [3]

Woodruff was an excellent fly fisherman and probably the first recorded to have fished with a fly west of the Continental Divide and in Idaho. His log indicated that on June 11, 1870 he fished the Blackfoot River and that in July of 1871 he fly fished in the Soda Springs, Idaho area. [4] While Woodruff fly fished in the southeastern part of Idaho, Will Carlin recorded his central Idaho fly fishing experiences in the late 1800s. Carlin was from New York and he and his hunting party journeyed from Spokane, Washington to Kendrick, Idaho in the Clearwater River area and then on into the Bitterroot Mountains by way of the Lolo Trail. Carlin was a skilled hunter and fly fisherman. On the Lolo and outside Weippe, Idaho, Carlin noted a fly fishing experience on September 20, 1893:

Carlin got out his tackle kit and took some line and a book of flies down to the creek...Carlin cut a willow switch some seven feet long, tied a few feet of line to the small end of it, and attached one of his flies. He cast into the middle of the creek and had a trout on his line as soon as the fly touched the water. He guessed the trout to weigh about a pound and a half. He cast again, and again a fish hit the fly immediately. Carlin continued to cast his fly upon the creek, and when he returned to the cabin after about an hour he had fifty-three fish weighing between a half pound and a pound and a half... [5]

Idaho became a state in 1890 with a population of over 88,000 people. During the late 1890s and early 1900s sportsmen from outside Idaho began buying land so that they might have fishing and hunting privileges in remote areas. The Island Park area of Fremont County, where Henry's Lake and Henry's Fork of the Snake River are located, became a favorite for sportsmen and ranchers. George Rea homesteaded the Shotgun Valley in 1878 and established a fish farm on his ranch. Robert Osborne also established a fish farm on his ranch in the same area. A.S. Trude bought the Arangee Land and Cattle Company in 1890 and the Rea Ranch in 1903. Trude was a true conservationist in his day and is also credited with having a fly named after him even though it was tied by Carter Harrison, the mayor of Chicago. [6] The "Trude" fly (and Trude style of tying) is the forerunner of the "Sofa Pillow" and "Elk Hair Caddis." To this day the Trude pattern is a favorite on many Idaho streams.

The Island Park Land and Cattle Company (IPL&CC) was not only a working ranch owned by railroad magnets William Bancroft and Silas Eccles but it was also a sportsman's retreat for fishing and hunting on the Henry's Fork of the Snake River. The Railroad Ranch, as it was called, eventually became the property of the Guggenheim and Harriman families.

Golden and Silver Lakes and the small creek that joins them, along with a major portion of the Henry's Fork, were the "private preserve" of the owners and their many guests. In 1902, fly fishing was the preferred method of angling for the great cutthroat, rainbow, brook trout, and grayling found in the waters on the ranch.

The land owners worked hard to persuade Idaho Fish and Game officials to protect the resource with special regulations. In 1950 some regulations were put into place but it was not until the 1970s, under the direction of Governor Cecil Andrus, that some stream sections were given serious protective regulations by the appointed commission of Pete Thompson, Jack Hemingway, Wynn Blake, Jack Alvord, and Will Godfrey.

The Railroad Ranch became the property of the state when the Roland and Averill Harriman families made a donation in 1978 to establish Harriman State Park. The agreement included special provisions, not only for hunting and ranching, but also for fly fishing on the famed waters.[7] Today, the general public enjoys this remarkable fishery with rod and fly, chasing after magnificent rainbows that inhabit the world renowned river.

It was in 1902 when another of Idaho's famous streams, Silver Creek, began to attract attention from fly fishermen around the world. As the story is told, J.J. Hardy of Alnwick, England wanted to fish the world's ten greatest trout streams before he died. He was the owner of Hardy Brothers, a very famous angling supply specialist. Harry C. Shellworth of Boise entertained Hardy on Silver Creek: "We all went to the stream by buckboards and the fishing was so good we could have filled a gunny sack in half an hour. Mr. Hardy was pleased."[8]

Silver Creek, like the Railroad Ranch of the Henry's Fork, gained in fame as noted people began to fish its waters for rainbow trout. The Hemingway family, especially the late Jack Hemingway, helped to bring recognition to this south central Idaho stream. Taylor "Bear Tracks" Williams is credited with fly fishing Silver Creek and the Little Wood and Big Wood Rivers in the 1920s. His fame lives on today as the developer of the traditional "Renegade" fly.[9]

The development of various organizations and clubs also helped to protect Idaho fisheries. While these organizations had the protection of hunting and fishing in mind, they were often organized to set aside the resource for private use. The North Fork Club, organized in the 1890s by well-to-do members of the Alta Club from Salt Lake City, began as a fishing, hunting, and card playing retreat. Some of the members wanted the club to be a stag operation but those who wanted to include wives and kids prevailed. The "losers" organized the Flat Rock Club.[10]

Henry Stampp sold his property located south of Highway 191 on the Henry's Fork of the Snake River to the Flat Rock Club. This club was also a fly fishing and hunting retreat and most of its members were from the Salt Lake City area by way of Spencer, Idaho.[11] The Tracy Club was located on Henry's Fork and its founder was also a former member of the North Fork Club. Tracy was from a Salt Lake City, Utah banking family and spent time with his father on the property as early as 1884.[12] Members of these clubs applied more than moral persuasion to protect the Henry's Fork and Sheridan area fisheries.

Other organizations that helped protect fisheries and the forest included the Utaida Club and the Coffee Pot Organization on the Henry's Fork. The Frontier Club of central Idaho and the Idaho Wildlife Federation also added their support to the idea that Idaho was a special place for those who enjoyed the highest quality hunting and fishing.

THE IDEA OF THE HENRY'S FORK FOUNDATION WAS ORIGINALLY DISCUSSED BY BILL MENLOVE OF PINE HAVEN, IDAHO AND FLY FISHING OUTFITTER AND FISH AND GAME COMMISSIONER WILL GODFREY DURING THE MID 1970S. THE FOUNDATION WAS ORGANIZED BY MENLOVE, MIKE LAWSON, AND OTHERS TO LOOK AFTER THE WELL-BEING OF THE LARGER UPPER SNAKE RIVER WATERSHED AND TO WORK WITH THE VARIOUS PARTIES THAT HAVE CLAIM TO OR IMPACT THE FLOW OF WATER IN THE HENRY'S FORK OF THE SNAKE RIVER. OVER THE YEARS THE FOUNDATION HAS ACCOMPLISHED A GREAT DEAL WITH ITS RESEARCH AND STREAM PROTECTION. THE FOUNDATION IS STILL IN OPERATION TODAY AND CONTINUES TO BE A VALUABLE FORCE IN PROTECTING THE RIVER.[13]

WITH THE 1965 ORGANIZATION OF THE FEDERATION OF FLY FISHERMEN, A NATIONAL ORGANIZATION, MORE CLUBS BEGAN TO FORM IN VARIOUS IDAHO COMMUNITIES. THE FIRST WAS THE BOISE VALLEY FLY FISHERMEN ORGANIZED BY KEN MAGEE, MARV TAYLOR, AND WILL GODFREY IN 1971. THIS CLUB HELPED TO SPAWN THE UPPER SNAKE RIVER FLY CASTERS OF REXBURG AND A CLUB AT TWIN FALLS. SOON THE KELLY CREEK FLY CASTERS OF LEWISTON, THE CLEARWATER FLY CASTERS IN MOSCOW, AND THE SNAKE RIVER CUTTHROAT CLUB WERE FORMED. ALL OF THESE CLUBS HELPED TO PROMOTE FLY FISHING AND PROTECT AND ENHANCE IDAHO'S MAGNIFICENT FISHERY RESOURCES IN THE '70S, '80S, AND '90S.

IN THE MID 1970S, GOVERNOR CECIL ANDRUS APPOINTED THE FISH AND GAME COMMISSION OF PETE THOMPSON, KEITH STONEBRAKER, JACK HEMINGWAY, DICK SWARZ, AND WILL GODFREY. THIS COMMISSION SET ABOUT TO PROTECT AND ENHANCE SEVERAL WILD TROUT FISHERIES IN THE STATE. WITH THE INFLUENCE OF STACY GEBHART (FISHERIES CHIEF), HERB POLLARD (FISHERIES), AND JOE GREENLEE (DIRECTOR), THEY ESTABLISHED SPECIAL METHODS REGULATIONS, NUMBER AND SIZE OF FISH THAT COULD BE HARVESTED, AND THE REMOVAL OF STATE GOVERNMENT FISH PLANTINGS. THESE REGULATIONS APPLIED INITIALLY TO THE RAILROAD RANCH AND BOX CANYON OF THE HENRY'S FORK, SILVER CREEK, KELLY CREEK, ST. JOE, AND LOCHSA RIVERS.

IDAHO FLY FISHING WAS GROWING ON MANY FRONTS THAT WERE MOSTLY UNCONNECTED IN THE EARLY DAYS. COMMUNICATION WAS SLOW AND TRAVEL WAS COMPLICATED. IT MAY HAVE BEEN WRITERS WHO HELP TO MOLD IDAHO'S REPUTATION FOR QUALITY FLY FISHING FROM THE 1930S THROUGH THE '50S. IDAHO NATIVE TED TRUEBLOOD MADE A MAJOR CONTRIBUTION TO THE DEVELOPMENT OF FLY FISHING WHEN HE WROTE SEVERAL BOOKS AND STORIES ABOUT FISHING AND HUNTING IN *FIELD AND STREAM* MAGAZINE. TRUEBLOOD WAS AN OUTDOORSMAN AND CONSIDERED TO BE A REAL "MAN'S MAN" WHEN IT CAME TO FLY FISHING. HIS FAME STILL PERSISTS IN THE SENIOR FISHING AND HUNTING ESTABLISHMENT TODAY. EVEN YOUNG FISHERMEN REVERE HIS CONTRIBUTIONS TO THE SPORT.[14]

THE INDUSTRY ALSO GREW THROUGH THE DEVELOPMENT OF SPECIALIZED FLY FISHING SHOPS AND GUIDE SERVICES. ALMA KUNZ, A DAIRY FARMER IN THE TETON VALLEY OF IDAHO, IS REPORTED TO HAVE TAKEN A RAILROAD EMPLOYEE FLY FISHING ON THE TETON RIVER IN 1919. THAT EVENT REPRESENTED THE START OF ALMA'S COMMERCIAL FLY FISHING LIFE. ALMA AND HIS BROTHER LYLE DEVELOPED A FLY FISHING OUTFITTER AND GUIDE BUSINESS IN THE 1930S NAMED ALMA'S LODGE. THIS COMPANY OPERATES TODAY AS THE TETON VALLEY LODGE.[15]

HARVEY AND MARCELLA OSWALD ESTABLISHED A SPORTING GOODS BUSINESS IN IDAHO FALLS IN 1944. MARCELLA LEARNED TO TIE FLIES, INCLUDING THE "MARCELLA TROUT FLY." THIS FLY AND MANY OF HER CREATIONS CARRIED THE OSWALD NAME INTO FLY FISHING CIRCLES TODAY. TWO OTHER QUALITY FLY FISHING SHOPS ALSO CAME INTO BEING DURING THE '30S AND '40S. RUEL STAINER'S FAMOUS RETAIL OUTLET IN TWIN FALLS AND DICK ALF'S SHOP IN KETCHUM, IDAHO WERE REVERED BY EXPERTS AND BEGINNERS ALIKE.

STAINER'S SHOP COULD, WITHOUT ANY ARGUMENT, BE CONSIDERED A "LANDFILL" OF HOOKS, FEATHERS, AND FLY FISHING SUPPLIES. STAINER WAS RENOWNED AS FLY FISHERMAN. ANGLERS TRAVELED LONG DISTANCES TO COME TO HIS SHOP, PICK UP A FEW ITEMS, AND LISTEN TO THE LATEST FISHING STORIES. HE IS THE CREATOR OF THE "STAINER DUCKTAIL," A FLY THAT EVEN TODAY IS REVERED AS ONE OF THE BEST FLIES FOR IDAHO LAKES.

FISH HATCHERY STEELHEAD
STANLEY, IDAHO

By contrast, the Dick Alf fly shop in Ketchum was a neat, well stocked fly fishing center for the residents of Sun Valley and its international clientele. Terry Ring, a very accomplished fly fisher, outfitter, businessman, and photographer purchased Alf's shop and runs it today as Silver Creek Outfitters.

Back in 1949, Buell Warner established the South Fork Lodge on the South Fork of the Snake River near Swan Valley and guided fly fishermen for $5 an hour. Ted Trueblood was one of Warner's regular clients. Spence Warner took over the business in 1976 and recently sold it. The South Fork Lodge is a viable fly fishing business today, owned by the Rockefeller family and managed by Mike and Shaun Lawson.

Fly fishing growth in the eastern part of Idaho was furthered by wealthy ranch and landowners and was also influenced by people coming to fish in Yellowstone Park. Sam Eagle and Alex Stuart opened a general store in West Yellowstone in 1908. The store featured general merchandise including cane fly rods, silk fly lines, gut leaders, and snelled flies. While most customers came to fly fish in Yellowstone Park, many traveled a few miles to the west to fish the Henry's Lake and Henry's Fork of the Snake River.

Eventually, Pat Barnes and Bud Lilly, both schoolteachers, established fly fishing guide services. Both the Barnes and Lilly fly shops became world renowned. Each eventually held fly fishing outfitter privileges on the Henry's Fork and Railroad Ranch. During the late '50s and early '60s, Walley Welch sold fly fishing supplies out of Max Inn in Island Park, Idaho. However, the first specialized fly fishing shop on the Henry's Fork was established by Will Godfrey.

Godfrey was a guide for Bud Lilly in 1965 and 1966. He spent a lot of his time guiding fly fishermen on the Henry's Fork, mainly Box Canyon, Railroad Ranch, and the river down to Ashton, Idaho. The training Lilly gave to Godfrey proved to be the inspiration that allowed Godfrey and his business partner George Wright to start the first fly fishing outfitter headquarters on the Henry's Fork at the famed Railroad Ranch in 1967. The Will Godfrey Fly Fishing Center was sold in 1986. Today the shop location is occupied by the Three Rivers Company and is represented by the Orvis Company.

Through Godfrey's efforts, many world class fly fishermen came to the Henry's Fork to sample the great rainbows found on the Railroad Ranch. Joe Brooks, Lee and Joan Wulff, Pete Hidy, Earnie Schwiebert, Keith Stonebraker, Tom Morgan, Jack Hemingway, Dan Callaghan, Lew Bell, Bill Nelson, Bing Lempke, and Stu Apt were among the notable fly fishers to experience this great river. Godfrey guided Dr. Carl Richards and Doug Swisher as they developed *Selective Trout*, a book about naturals and fly tying.[16] Charles Kroll spent many days with Godfrey as he gathered information for his book about brook trout entitled *Squaretail*.[17] *Fly Fisherman* magazine featured several articles about the Henry's Fork and the Godfrey Fly Fishing Center during the 1970s.

In 1972 Mike Lawson organized Henry's Fork Anglers and established a second fly fishing outfitter and guide business at Last Chance on the Henry's Fork. Lawson, an accomplished fly fisher, guide, and author operates today on the Henry's Fork and the South Fork of the Snake River. Since those early days, others have come to the Henry's Fork with their tackle shops and guide services. René Harrop and his investor group organized the Trout Hunter Company and the Hyde Company established their operation at Last Chance, Idaho.

While fly fishing was developing in eastern and south central Idaho at a rapid pace, the northern regions of Idaho also grew popular. Beyond trout fishing on the Selway, Lochsa, St. Joe, St. Mary's, Coeur d'Alene, and Moyie, there was a developing interest in catching salmon and steelhead with a fly. Salmon and steelhead migrate from the Pacific Ocean through the Columbia River and into Idaho via the Snake River each year.

While early salmon and steelhead fly fishing developed in Oregon and Washington, chasing these magnificent fish with a fly soon took hold in Idaho on the Clearwater, Snake, and Salmon Rivers.

In the early days it was thought that a steelhead or salmon would not take a fly. It is generally accepted that Bill Nelson of Eugene, Oregon was the first to try and catch a steelhead on a fly on the Clearwater River of Idaho during the mid-1940s when he was a student at Washington State University. Ted Trueblood and Dr. John Carsow of Lewiston also engaged in steelhead fly fishing on the Clearwater.[18]

Perk Lyda was the first guide and outfitter on the Clearwater to take fly fishermen, establishing his business in 1963. Keith Stonebraker was an avid fly fisher for steelhead in the early 1960s as was Bill Alspach in the 1970s. Alspach is credited with the development of a famous steelhead fly called "Beats Me."[19] Jeff Jarrett followed in the footsteps of Lyda by establishing a fly fishing guide service for steelhead in the '70s.

Today, runs of wild steelhead are protected, while hatchery or "government" steelhead make up the majority of fish in the runs. Hells Canyon Dam on the Snake River and the Dworshak Dam on the North Fork of the Clearwater River were deathly for any fish returning to upstream spawning grounds. There was no way around the two dams. Mitigation in the form of federal, state, and Indian hatcheries help encourage the runs of steelhead and salmon today. A strong movement exists to remove lower Snake River dams as they are a major deterrent to spawning fish returning to Idaho. The battles are being fought in the courts by environmental groups, Rivers United, Salmon Coalition, and others as they try to convince electrical energy, agriculture, developers, and the general public that these fish runs of salmon and steelhead are important.

Fly fishing from a floating device other than a boat was not invented in Idaho but it certainly was perfected on Idaho waters. Ruel Stainer and Marshall Everhart enjoyed many evenings of fishing below Magic Dam on the Wood River using a float tube in the early 1950s. However, perfection in using the device is credited to Nampa's Darrell Grimm. He added the use of scuba flippers as a means for propulsion as well as the stripping apron and the back rest. The use and promotion of float tubes moved the sport forward when the Boise Valley Fly Fishermen, under the direction of Ken Magee, became "Idaho's Fly Fishing Navy" in the 1970s. Word got out and the float tube fly fishing industry took off nationwide.

Today, fly fishing in Idaho for all species of trout, steelhead, salmon, bass, crappie, blue gill, and carp has become a well developed sport. There are plenty of specialized fly shops. Guides and outfitters for fly fishing abound on most every river. Articles and books promoting Idaho and fly fishing are in abundance. Fly tying expositions, casting contests, conservation work, and clubs all actively promote the sport of fly fishing.

Much of the future of continued excellent Idaho fly fishing lies in teaching young people about the sport and all of its nuances. Clayne Baker has been at the forefront of such an effort by organizing the Woolley Buggers, an Idaho fly fishing youth organization. The program's motto is "There's more to fishing than catching fish," and more than 600 youths have passed through it, learning about sportsmanship and character. The goal is to teach kids to enjoy the environment and also think about how to make it better and preserve it.[20]

It is very possible that one of the rivers than ran east out of Eden was in Idaho. Adam and Eve may have enjoyed the great drake mayfly hatch on a favorite river, just as fly fishers from around the world enjoy the more than 15,000 miles of major stream flow in Idaho, not to mention the thousands of miles of small creeks that have less notoriety. Idaho is certainly the place to be if you are searching for the "Eden" of fly fishing.

EASTERN IDAHO

EASTERN IDAHO AS A FLY FISHING MECCA CAME INTO ITS OWN IN THE 1970S, EVEN THOUGH MANY OF THE RIVERS, STREAMS, AND LAKES HAD BEEN EXPLORED AND MAPPED IN THE EARLY 1800S. SOME OF THE BEST FLY SHOPS AND GUIDE SERVICES IN THE WEST ARE LOCATED IN THIS AREA. EACH HAS A LONG HISTORY OF SERVICE TO THE NOVICE AND ADVANCED FLY ANGLER. HENRY'S FORK OF THE SNAKE RIVER WAS NAMED AFTER THE EXPLORER ANDREW HENRY. THE SECTIONS OF THE RIVER KNOWN AS BOX CANYON AND RAILROAD RANCH ATTRACT FLY FISHERS FROM AROUND THE WORLD. THERE ARE AT LEAST TEN IMPORTANT MAYFLY AND STONEFLY HATCHES, NOT TO MENTION A WIDE VARIETY OF CADDIS THAT SERVE AS THE FOOD SOURCE FOR THE MIGHTY RAINBOWS OF THE HENRY'S FORK. IMPORTANT SCENIC AREAS INCLUDE BIG MESA FALLS AND CARDIAC CANYON, BUT FOR SECLUSION, THE AREA BETWEEN RIVERSIDE AND SHEEP FALLS IS BEST.

THE SOUTH FORK OF THE SNAKE RIVER IS KNOWN FOR ITS GREAT CUTTHROAT TROUT, OCCASIONAL TROPHY BROWN TROUT, AND A SCATTERING OF RAINBOW TROUT. THE SOUTH FORK IS A WONDERFUL DRY FLY STREAM. THIS GREAT RIVER IS BEST FISHED FROM A DRIFT BOAT. THE TETON RIVER IS LOCATED ON THE WEST SLOPE OF THE TETON MOUNTAINS AND IS A MEANDERING MEADOW-LIKE STREAM. GREAT HATCHES AND CUT BANKS PROVIDE A HABITAT FOR RAINBOW AND CUTTHROAT TROUT. THE FALLS RIVER IS A FREE-STONE STREAM FLOWING TO THE WEST OUT OF THE SOUTHWESTERN SECTION OF YELLOWSTONE PARK. THIS COLD, CLEAR STREAM IS THE HOME OF SOME MIGHTY STRONG RAINBOWS. IT IS ALSO A SLIPPERY RIVER AND REQUIRES ANGLERS TO BE PREPARED WITH STAFF AND CLEAT.

THE BLACKFOOT AND PORTNEUF RIVERS ARE EASILY OVERLOOKED BECAUSE OF THE FAME OF THE MORE NORTHERN STREAMS. THESE TWO CUTTHROAT AND RAINBOW TROUT STREAMS ARE SMALLER AND FLOW THROUGH THE QUIET COUNTRYSIDE. THE PORTNEUF RUNS CLEAR IN THE SUMMER AND THE EVENING HATCHES ARE MAGNIFICENT. THIS STREAM IS KNOWN TO PRODUCE SOME LARGER FISH ON THE FLY.

EASTERN IDAHO IS ALSO ENDOWED WITH A NUMBER OF PRODUCTIVE SMALL CREEKS. BITCH CREEK, ROBINSON CREEK, PALISADES CREEK, WARM RIVER, FOX CREEK, AND MEDICINE LODGE CREEK ARE NUMBERED AMONG THE BEST. MOST ALWAYS FREQUENTED BY LOCALS, THESE SMALLER, BRUSHY, FREE-STONE STREAMS OFFER THE ANGLER A FUN VARIETY OF TROUT.

THE LAKES AND RESERVOIRS OF EASTERN IDAHO HAVE THEIR OWN STRONG REPUTATIONS. AMONG THE MANY BODIES OF WATER THAT PRODUCE GREAT FLY FISHING IS HENRY'S LAKE. VERY LARGE HYBRID CUTTHROAT TROUT AND BROOK TROUT ARE THE FEATURED FISH. FLY FISHING IN JUNE AND EARLY JULY CAN BE GREAT. HOWEVER, IN AUTUMN THE BROOK TROUT BECOME VERY ACTIVE.

ISLAND PARK RESERVOIR, PALISADES RESERVOIR, CHESTERFIELD LAKE, BLACKFOOT RESERVOIR, AND 24 MILE RESERVOIR REPRESENT IDEAL FLY FISHING EXPERIENCES FOR THOSE WHO ENJOY FLOAT TUBE FLY FISHING. EARLY MORNING AND EVENING HATCHES BRING OUT THE BEST FISH.

EARLY MORNING
TETON RIVER

THE TETONS

FARMING NEAR THE TETON MOUNTAINS

Previous Page:
Bend in the River
Teton River

Water
Teton River

The Banks of the Teton
Teton River

Early Morning Fog
Teton River

STREET SIGN
TETON RIVER

HENRY'S FORK FAN

RAINBOW TROUT

DILLON WITMER
HENRY'S LAKE

CAMPING ON THE HENRY'S FORK

HENRY'S FORK
BRETT HARTLEY

Prevous page:
Morning Hatch
Henry's Fork

Henry's Fork Spring
Henry's Fork

CAUTION ANGLERS

WATCH FOR ACTIVE GROUND
NESTING IN THIS AREA
MAY THROUGH AUGUST
THANK YOU
HARRIMAN STATE PARK
HENRYS FORK FOUNDATION

MESA FALLS
HENRY'S FORK

MESA FALLS OF THE HENRY'S FORK
DILLON WITMER

TRICKY WADE
MESA FALLS OF THE HENRY'S FORK

NEAR THE FALLS
DILLON WITMER
MESA FALLS OF THE HENRY'S FORK

WARM RIVER
BRETT HARTLEY

FALL RIVER
BRETT HARTLEY

SPRING
SOUTH FORK OF THE SNAKE

SOUTH FORK OF THE SNAKE

THE LODGE AT PALISADES CREEK
SOUTH FORK OF THE SNAKE

SOUTH FORK OF THE BOISE

ROD RACK
SOUTH FORK OF THE SNAKE

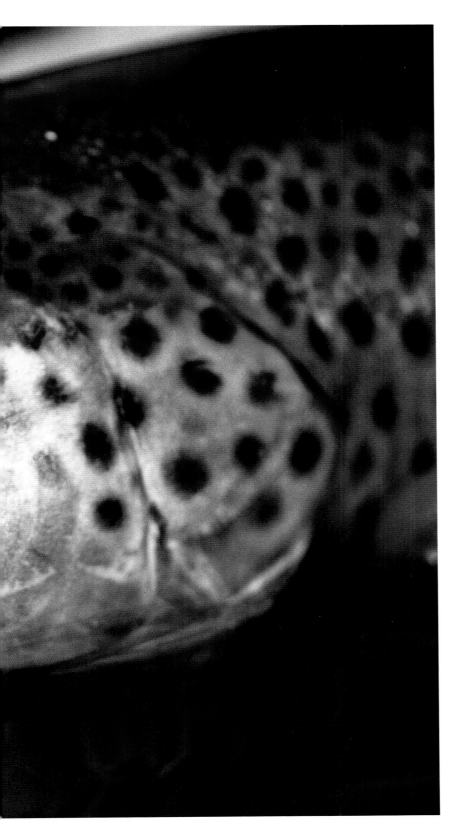

Brown Trout

Mayfly
Calibetas

PORTNEUF RIVER

MEDICINE LODGE CREEK

MEDICINE LODGE CREEK

24 Mile Reservoir
Chesterfield

MEDICINE LODGE
CREEK

Central Idaho

The Salmon River is the primary attraction in Central Idaho. This great river begins in the Sawtooth and Smoky Mountains and flows north through Stanley, Challis, and on to the town of Salmon. It is at this point that the great river bends to the west and heads into Idaho's north central area. The river picks up volume from literally hundreds of springs, creeks, and major tributaries. The East Salmon, Pashimeroi, Yankee Fork, Williams Creek, Lemhi, and many more feed this great river. Fly fishing on the upper Salmon River offers steelhead and some native species. The salmon runs of the past are very endangered and only a few fish make it back to Redfish Lake.

There are also other rivers in this region that head south to meet the Snake River. The Big Lost and Little Lost Rivers are named in such a way as to depict their flow, which sinks deep into the middle Snake River Plain aquifer. The Big Lost becomes "lost" somewhere in the Arco desert emerging, many think, at Thousand Springs in the Hagerman Valley.

The Big Lost is formed by several creeks including Wildhorse, East, West, and North Forks, and Summit Creek. The Boulder and Pioneer Mountains, some of the highest in the state of Idaho, catch the snow that eventually melts and becomes the Big Lost. Copper Basin, near the head of the East and West Forks, has taken the brunt of the fly fishing pressure. Some say that the fishing in the area is not what it used to be. Perhaps this is due to the pressure from those traveling over Trail Creek Pass from the Wood River Valley; perhaps it is because Idaho Fish and Game has a policy of planting government fish on top of wild populations; perhaps disease from the hatcheries has been the culprit. Even so, this popular area, including the Mackay Reservoir tailwaters, is a wonderful place to fish.

A little to the north and east of the Big Lost River is the Little Lost River Valley. The stream that flows toward the south is the Little Lost. While this stream is overshadowed by many other premier Idaho rivers and creeks, the tributary known as Sawmill Creek can be productive for some nice rainbow and brook trout.

On the west side of central Idaho, the fly fisherman will encounter the Payette River system which includes the South, Middle, and North Fork stretches. Fly fishers flock to Long Valley and the Payette Lakes as well as the Alpine Lakes outside of McCall. The management of many of these lakes is for trophy trout. Fly fishing at Blackwell, Long, Louie, Brush, and Crystal Lakes, as well as Lake Serene is regulated by size, quantity, and method of fishing. Some family fly fishing can be secured at Cascade Reservoir, often referred to as the most utilized fishery in Idaho. Expect trout and bass to be taken in this 30,000-acre lake located south of McCall near the town of Cascade. The entire Payette drainage represents hundreds of creeks and rivers. Trips can be made by hiking, flying in, guided or unguided day trips, or pack trips that last for a week or more.

Many fly fishers also enjoy Warm Lake east of Cascade as well as the Sagehen, Deadwood, and Horsethief Reservoirs, all found in central Idaho near Cascade. These float tube bodies of water provide added excitement to any Idaho fly fishing adventure.

Winter
Big Lost River

Previous Page:
Lost River Range

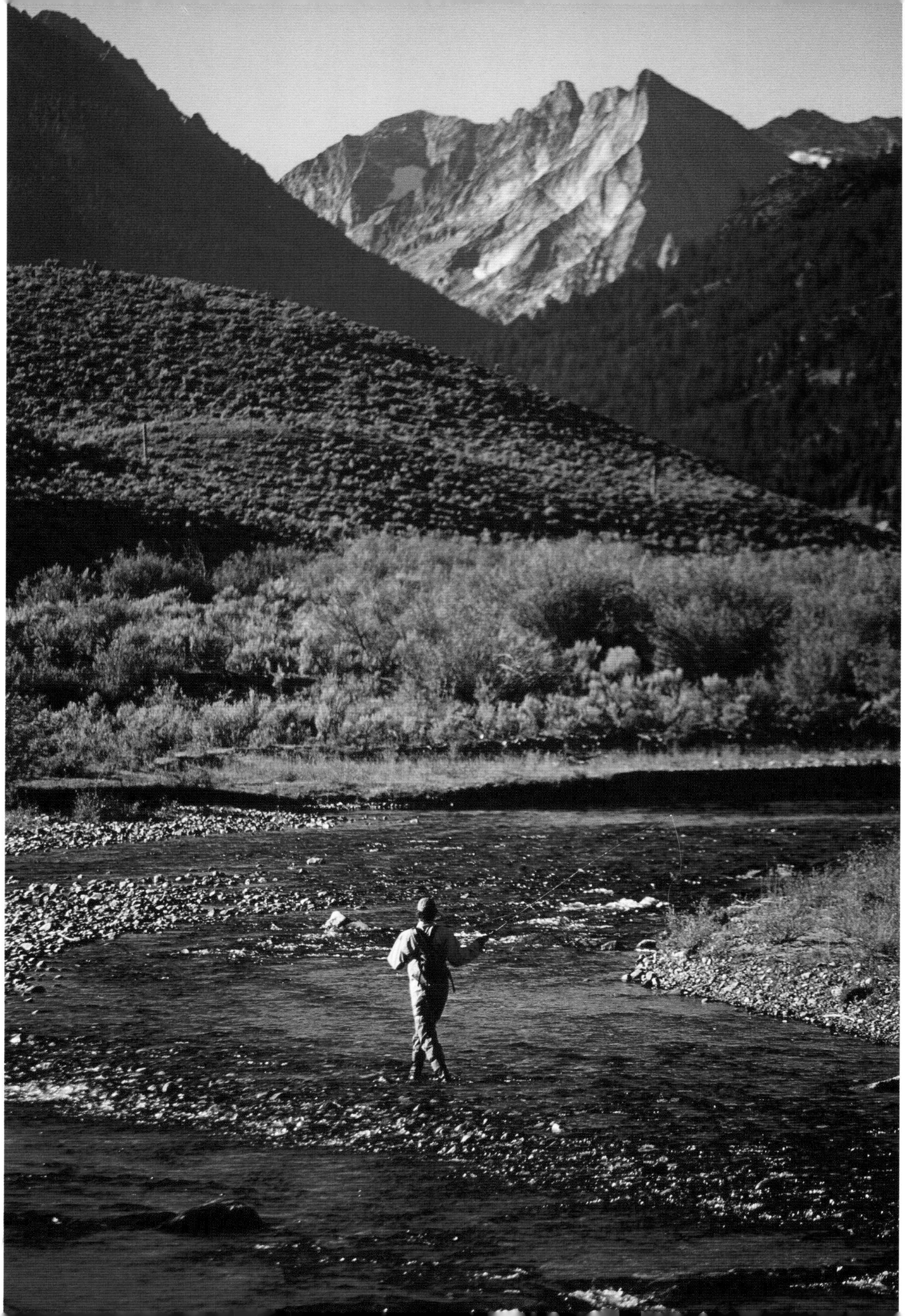

Wild Horse Creek
Dave James
Copper Basin

EAST FORK OF THE BIG LOST
DAVE JAMES
COPPER BASIN

IN FOCUS
BIG LOST RIVER

Previous page:
Copper Basin
Dave James

Copper Basin

Copper Basin

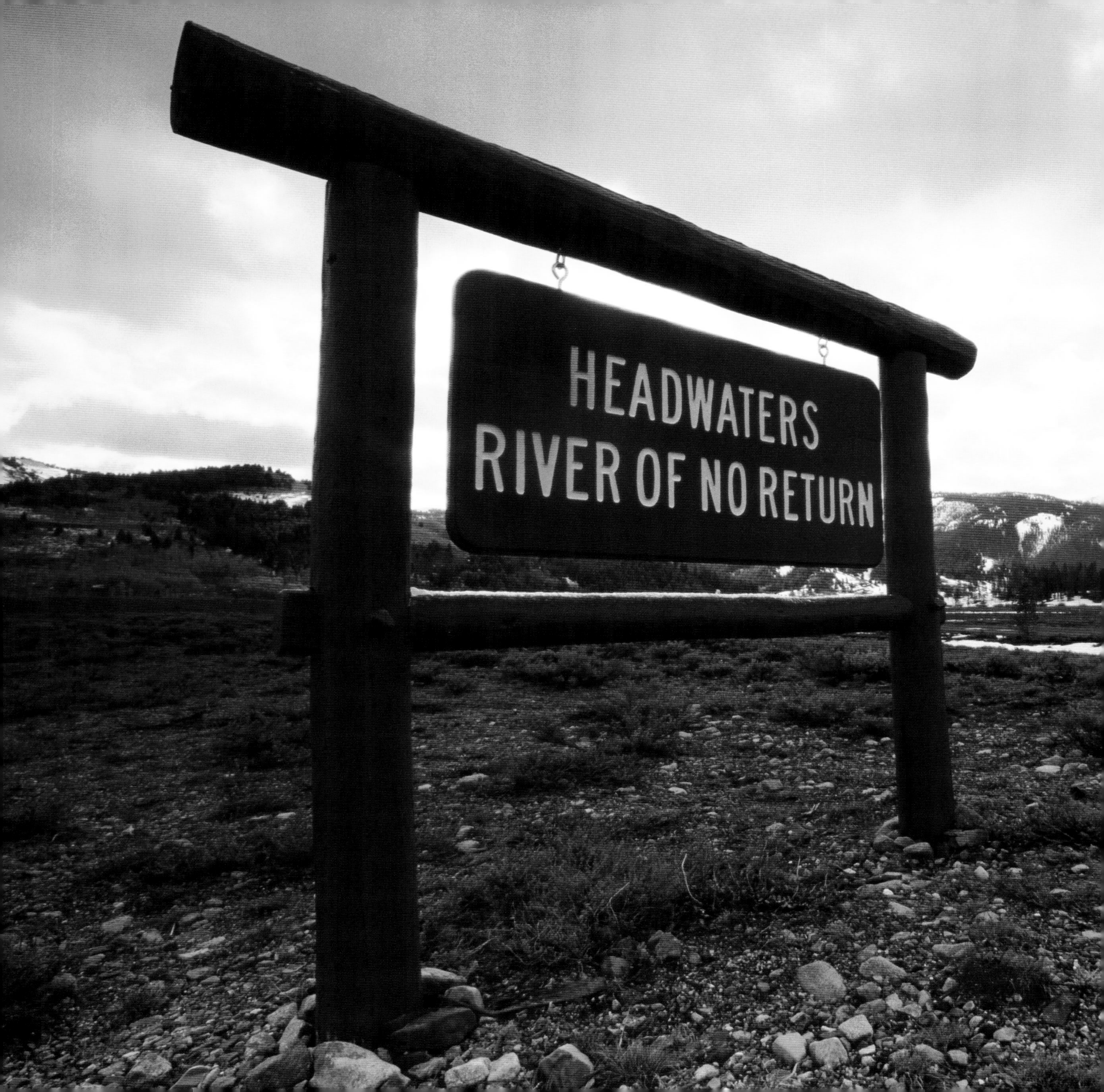
HEADWATERS
RIVER OF NO RETURN

SALMON RIVER

SALMON RIVER
HEADWATERS

SALMON RIVER
JOHN ASHTON

SALMON RIVER
JASON BUCK, BRYANT DUNN,
AND SCOTT CRABTREE

STANLEY, IDAHO

**WAPITI MEADOW
RANCH**
JUSTIN JORDAN
EAST FORK OF THE
SOUTH FORK OF THE
SALMON

**WAPITI MEADOW
RANCH
JOHNSON CREEK**
JUSTIN JORDAN

WAITING FOR ACTION
WAPITI MEADOW RANCH

WINTER STEELHEAD
SCOTT CRABTREE
SALMON RIVER

SOUTH CENTRAL/WESTERN IDAHO

FLY FISHERS ARE ALWAYS LOOKING FOR VARIETY AND SOUTH CENTRAL IDAHO IS BLESSED WITH A WIDE ASSORTMENT OF FLY FISHING WATERS. THE MOST FAMOUS IS SILVER CREEK. SILVER CREEK WILL CHALLENGE THE MOST KNOWLEDGEABLE, MOST SKILLED FLY ANGLER. THIS GREAT STREAM, KNOWN FOR ITS HIGHLY SELECTIVE RAINBOW AND BROWN TROUT, CAN MAKE THE BEST FLY FISHERS WONDER IF THEY NEED FURTHER SCHOOLING. LIKE THE GREAT HENRY'S FORK RAILROAD RANCH, SILVER CREEK IS AN ULTIMATE TEST IN FLY FISHING. THE WADING STALK, ACCURACY OF THE CAST, MATCHING THE HATCH, AND PRESENTING THE FLY REPRESENT THE CURRICULUM AND ONLY A FEW EARN A DEGREE.

ONCE SILVER CREEK DEPARTS THE WOOD RIVER VALLEY AT THE SOUTHEAST CORNER, IT JOINS WITH THE OBSCURE LITTLE WOOD RIVER. THE SCENERY CHANGES AND THE SYSTEM TURNS INTO GRASSHOPPER-INFESTED SAGE COUNTRY WITH A SPRINKLING OF AGRICULTURE. THE STREAM IS KNOWN TO HAVE PRODUCED SOME SIZEABLE BROWN TROUT. JACK HEMINGWAY LOVED TO FLY FISH THE LITTLE WOOD IN THE LATE AFTERNOON WITH A HOPPER FLY AND A LIGHT ROD.

TO THE NORTH, THE FLY FISHER CAN EXPERIENCE THE TUMBLING WATERS OF THE BIG WOOD RIVER. CUT BANKS, RIFFLES, POOLS, DEBRIS PILES, AND LONG RUNS ARE THE FEATURES OF THIS FINE CENTRAL IDAHO FREE-STONE STREAM. FLOWING IN A SOUTHWEST DIRECTION FROM KETCHUM TOWARD MAGIC RESERVOIR THROUGH THE WOOD RIVER VALLEY, THIS WONDERFUL STREAM OFFERS THE BEST IN DRY AND BEADHEAD DROPPER FLY FISHING. HATCHES ARE ABUNDANT AND THE STREAM OFFERS A WIDE VARIETY OF EXPERIENCES.

SOME STREAMS IN THIS PART OF IDAHO ARE OFTEN OVERLOOKED BECAUSE OF THE ATTRACTION OF SILVER CREEK AND THE BIG WOOD RIVER. AMONG THEM ARE THE BOISE RIVER AND ITS SOUTH FORK, MIDDLE FORK, AND NORTH FORK. THE DRAINAGES FOR EACH OF THESE STREAMS REPRESENT MILES AND MILES OF EXCELLENT FLY FISHING. THE APPROXIMATE 25 MILES OF FREE FLOW OF THE SOUTH FORK OF THE BOISE RIVER BETWEEN ANDERSON RANCH DAM AND THE ARROW ROCK DAM BACKWATERS IS LOADED WITH FAT RAINBOW TROUT. THE STRETCH BETWEEN DANSKIN BRIDGE AND NEAL BRIDGE, ABOUT 17 MILES LONG, IS ACCOMPLISHED BY FLOAT ONLY AND REQUIRES SOME SKILL TO NAVIGATE. THE FLY OF CHOICE IS USUALLY THE "PINK ALBERT" BUT THERE ARE MANY HATCHES FOR THE FLY FISHER TO MATCH. THE BEAUTY AND SOLITUDE OF THE BOISE RIVER DRAINAGE IS SPECTACULAR—HIGH DESERT WITH PATCHES OF PONDEROSA PINE.

THE MAIN SNAKE RIVER ALSO FLOWS THROUGH THIS PART OF IDAHO. THE FLY ANGLER SHOULD NOT PASS UP THE HAGERMAN VALLEY, THE BACKWATERS OF C.J. STRIKE RESERVOIR, OR THE FISHERIES IN AND AROUND THE BRUNEAU DUNES. CRANE FALLS, LITTLE VALLEY, AND THE PONDS AND LAKES OF DUCK VALLEY IN THE SOUTH ALL REPRESENT IDEAL FLOAT TUBE FLY FISHING EXPERIENCES. THIS IS ALL HIGH DESERT COUNTRY. IT HAS ITS OWN BEAUTY AND MYSTERY AND MOST OF THE TIME IT IS OVERLOOKED.

FALL
BIG WOOD RIVER

BIG WOOD RIVER
RYAN SKENE

Big Wood River
Ryan Skene and
Hank at day's end

BIG WOOD RIVER
DILLON WITMER

BIG WOOD RIVER
DILLON WITMER

BIG WOOD RIVER
SARAH PARKER

BIG WOOD RIVER
BRIAN BLIGH

BIG WOOD RIVER
RILEY BUCK

BIG WOOD RIVER
RILEY BUCK

BIG WOOD RIVER

BIG WOOD RIVER
RILEY BUCK

BIG WOOD RIVER
JOHN ASHTON IN THE MIDST OF A TRICO HATCH

PUTTING UP A FIGHT
RAINBOW TROUT

Brown Trout
Thatcher Marstead

Rainbow Trout

SILVER CREEK
REFLECTION OF SHELLY THORNTON

RIVER BANK

SILVER CREEK
SHELLY THORNTON

SILVER CREEK
JON MCGUONE

THE DAM
ANDERSON RANCH
RESERVOIR

ANDERSON RANCH
RESERVOIR

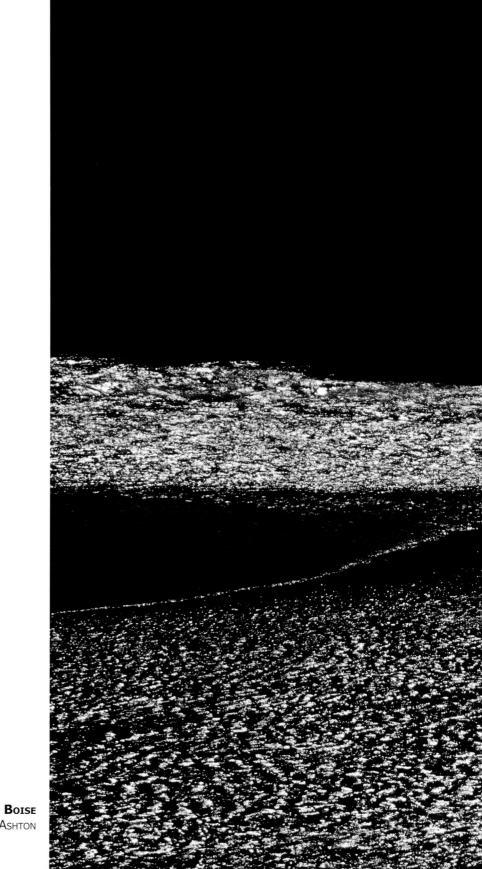

SOUTH FORK OF THE BOISE
JOHN ASHTON

SOUTH FORK OF THE BOISE
JOHN ASHTON

117

SOUTH FORK OF THE BOISE
WARBLER

**SOUTH FORK
OF THE BOISE**
SHAWN TIERNEY

**RAINBOW
TROUT**

North Central Idaho

The north central area fisheries of Idaho cover a lot of country. The region ranges from the Montana border in the east and the Lemhi River to the Oregon/Washington border in the west where the Salmon River meets the Snake River below Hell's Canyon.

The wild nature of the Middle Fork of the Salmon River is just spectacular. Over 100 miles of nearly inaccessible riverbank will challenge the very best fly fishermen. The stretch from Indian Creek to the confluence with the main Salmon River takes five days of floating, camping, and fly fishing. Camping at designated sites based on one's permit allows a few miles of travel each day. This river has special regulations that need to be checked annually. It is also a river for those who are skilled in handling rough water.

It is difficult to place the main stem of the Salmon River into a specific Idaho region. Its flow heads north out of the Sawtooth Mountains, just over Galena Pass from Sun Valley. Picking up the runoff from many smaller creeks, the Salmon gains size in its northern flow toward the town of Salmon. But here the "River of No Return" heads west and crosses the entire state to the town of Riggins where it turns north again. It winds for another 60 miles, through the Salmon River canyon, and unites with the mighty Snake River north of Hell's Canyon. The Salmon River is named for the great runs of salmon that used to come in from the Pacific Ocean via the Columbia and Snake Rivers. The wild salmon runs are nearly non-existent today and depend mostly on hatchery-bred fish. Steelhead from the Pacific Ocean, like the salmon, make their way over several high Snake River dams and into the river system during September and October of each year. These mighty steelhead provide a very exciting fly fishing experience up the entire Salmon River system from the Snake River confluence to Challis, Idaho. Single handed fly rodders as well as speycasters enjoy steelhead on a fly up to 12 pounds.

Lemhi River

FLOWING NORTH FROM NEAR LEADORE, IDAHO, THE LEMHI RIVER REACHES THE SALMON RIVER AT SALMON, IDAHO AFTER FLOWING THROUGH THE RANCHES AND FARMS OF THE WIDE LEMHI VALLEY. SPRINGS AND CREEKS FLOWING OFF THE EAST SIDE OF THE VALLEY AND THE LEMHI MOUNTAINS MEET THE STREAMS FLOWING EAST OUT OF THE CHALLIS SALMON NATIONAL FOREST TO FORM THE LEMHI RIVER. DURING THE 1970S THE LAST OF THE BIG SALMON RUNS MADE THEIR WAY UP THE LEMHI TO SPAWN. THE LEMHI TODAY IS A TROUT STREAM AND DURING THE LATE SUMMER A LOT OF THE WATER IS USED FOR AGRICULTURAL PURPOSES, MAKING IT SOMEWHAT OF A SUSPECT FISHERY.

THE SELWAY AND LOCHSA RIVERS FLOW OUT OF THE HIGH COUNTRY AND MEET AT LOWELL TO FORM THE MIDDLE FORK OF THE CLEARWATER. CUTTHROAT TROUT, SALMON, AND STEELHEAD ARE THE ATTRACTION IN THESE RIVERS FOR FLY FISHERMEN. STEELHEAD ENTER THE CLEARWATER SYSTEM AT LEWISTON AS EARLY AS JULY. THROUGH THE FALL AND ON INTO THE FOLLOWING SPRING FLY FISHERS CAN SWING A FLY FOR WILD AND HATCHERY STEELHEAD UP TO 20 POUNDS. DURING THE SPRING AND EARLY SUMMER SALMON MAKE THEIR WAY UP THE CLEARWATER SYSTEM INTO THE SOUTH FORK, SELWAY, AND LOCHSA. THE SPRING RUNOFF OCCURS DURING THAT TIME AND FISHING CAN BE TOUGH FOR THE FLY FISHERMAN.

THE SNAKE RIVER BELOW HELL'S CANYON IS A FISHERY BY BOAT. STEELHEAD IN THE FALL, SALMON IN THE SPRING, AND SMALL MOUTH BASS YEAR ROUND MAKE THIS A FLY FISHERMAN'S PARADISE. IT WOULD TAKE A LIFETIME TO FISH ALL THE WATERS OF NORTH CENTRAL IDAHO.

SELWAY RIVER

WAPITI MEADOW RANCH
MIDDLE FORK OF THE SALMON RIVER
INDIAN CREEK BACKCOUNTRY LANDING STRIP

AROUND THE RANGE
LOCHSA RIVER

MORNING
RIVERSCAPE
SELWAY RIVER

Northern Idaho

The northern section of the state is another world altogether. It is different than the high rolling farm lands and lodgepole pine forests of eastern Idaho; different than the high desert of central and south central Idaho; different than the meandering region of the Snake River through the southern part of the state. It is a maze of beauty that includes the rugged wilderness, northern drainages, huge lakes, tall red cedar forests, tamaracks, and great rivers.

The major trout fishing streams include the St. Joe, North Fork of the Clearwater, Kelly Creek, Weitas Creek, North Fork of the Coeur d'Alene, the Kootenai, St Mary's River, and the Moyie. There is enough free-flowing water in these streams to provide a fly caster with a lifetime of enjoyment. Some say that there is no need to go elsewhere.

Kelly Creek, high in the Clearwater National Forest, is a wonderful cutthroat trout stream with great hatches and clear water. As the major tributary to the North Fork of the Clearwater, Kelly Creek has special regulations that have preserved this wonderful fishery located deep in the forested canyons. Not to be outdone is the little-known Weitas Creek that flows into the North Fork of the Clearwater from the south. The North Fork is an absolutely beautiful river with a cutthroat trout behind every rock.

The St. Joe is a "must stream to fish" before one's fly fishing life comes to an end. Strong, fat cutthroat trout abound in this great stream where special regulations have made it one of Idaho's "Blue Ribbon" fly fishing streams. The upper river flows through tall red cedar forests. The St. Mary's River lies to the south and is not very well known because of the attention given to many of the special regulation waters of the region. The St. Mary's is a trout stream with decent hatches and reasonable access from up or downstream of Santa, Idaho.

If a large river is the desire, the Kootenai fits the bill. Flowing westward out of the area near Libby, Montana, this huge river cuts across the top of Idaho near Bonner's Ferry before it heads into Canada. This is a great float river and there are some very large trout to be taken with streamers and large bugs. While in the north, fly fishers should also try the Moyie—especially in the fall season.

The larger lakes and reservoirs of north Idaho turn the landscape into something resembling the northwest coast of Canada. Pend Oreille, Coeur d'Alene, and Priest Lakes, as well as Moose Creek Reservoir are all beautiful and mysterious. Each has its own unique fishery where major streams have their inflow and where a fly fisherman can be secluded in a cove or hidden bay. A float tube, canoe, or paddle boat will give the angler a chance at some rather hefty lake trout, kokanee salmon, rainbow, and cutthroat trout. The 23,000-acre Priest Lake gained fame as a result of the large lake trout inhabiting its waters 2,400 feet above sea level. Lake Pend Oreille covers several thousand acres and is known for its very large lake trout and rainbows. Just south of Sandpoint, Idaho lies the 800-acre Cocolalla Lake. Trout and many warm water species of fish including bass and crappie offer a fun variety for the fly fisherman who likes to fish from a float tube or flotation device. Moose Creek Reservoir is a mixed-species body of water. Bass, crappie, and rainbow trout are found in this 50-acre lake. Northern Idaho has it all and certainly represents the ultimate in fly fishing opportunities.

Priest Lake

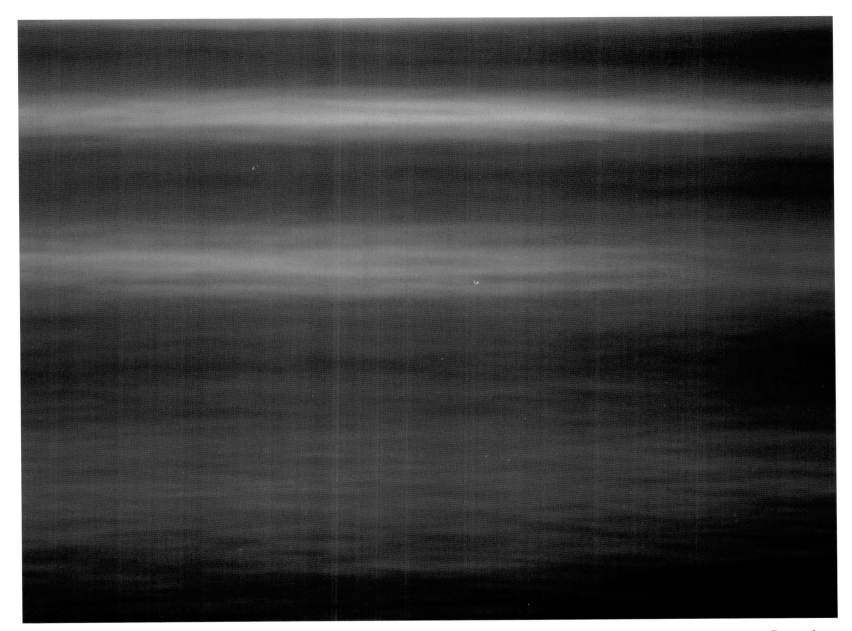

PRIEST LAKE

FOLIAGE
PRIEST LAKE

SAILBOAT
LAKE PEND ORIELLE

MOONLIGHT
HAYDEN LAKE

HAYDEN LAKE
PATRICK DUNN-BAKER

GOLDEN LIGHT
ST. JOE RIVER
ST. JOE LODGE

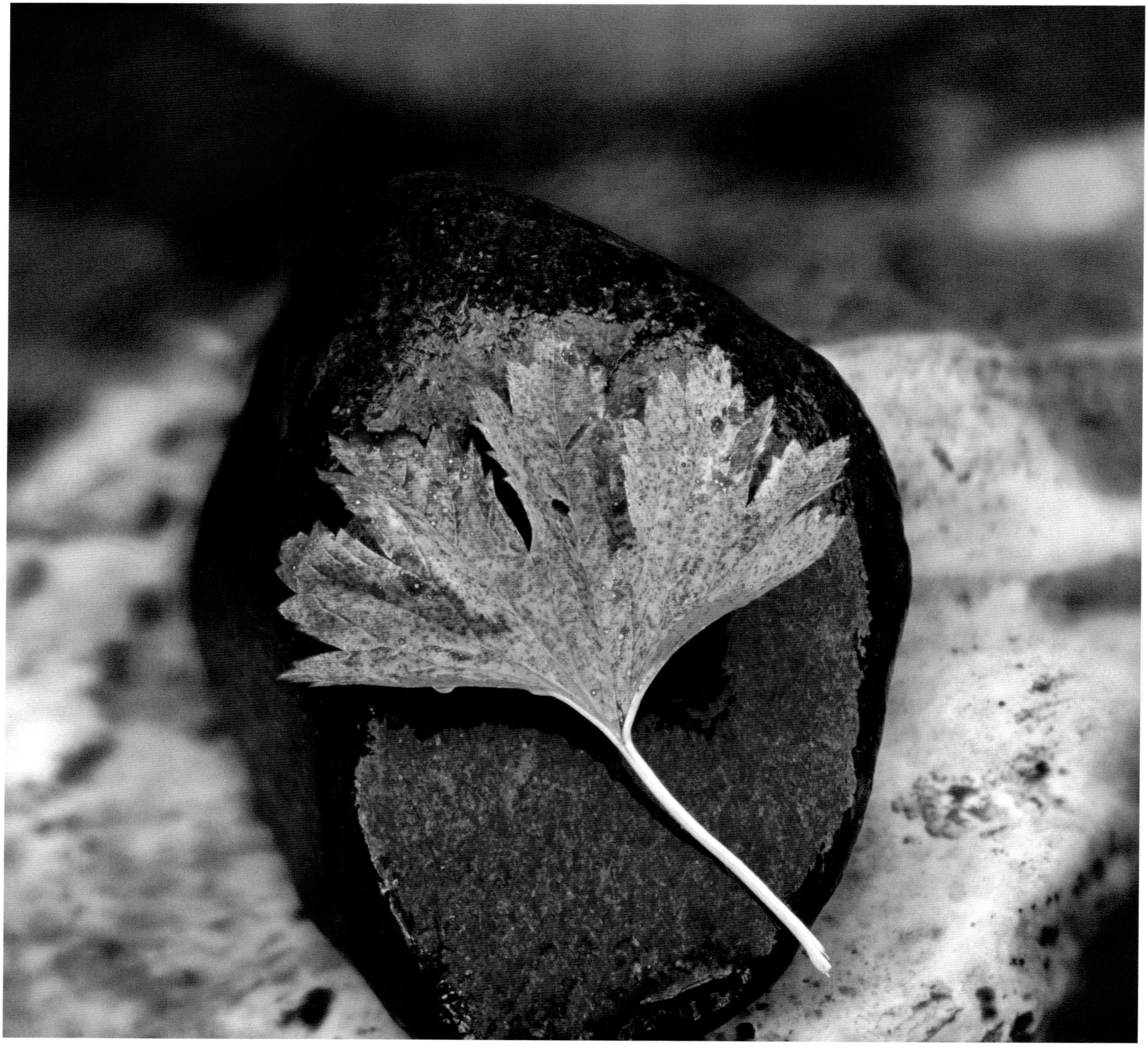

St. Joe River
St. Joe Lodge

St. Joe River

Packing In
St. Joe Lodge

St. Joe River
St. Joe Lodge Meadow

OLD RIVERFRONT CABIN
St. Joe River

ST. JOE RIVER
STEVE MORAN
ST. JOE LODGE

EVENING
MIKE WILSON
NORTH FORK OF THE COEUR D' ALENE

WESTERN LIGHT ON WEITAS CREEK
FLYING B RANCH

FLYING B RANCH
COREY SWANSON LEADS THE CREW
WEITAS CREEK

SLEEPING QUARTERS
WEITAS CREEK
FLYING B RANCH

FLYING B RANCH
WEITAS CREEK

FLYING B RANCH
WEITAS CREEK

KELLY CREEK

155

PREVIOUS
PAGE:
CLEARWATER
RIVER

SNAKE RIVER
DAVE FAULTINGS

SNAKE RIVER
DAVE FAULTINGS

MORNING MIST
CLEARWATER RIVER

NORTH FORK OF THE CLEARWATER RIVER

SNAKE RIVER
RIP FAULTINGS CAMPING

THANK YOU

To my family for their continued support and enduring belief in my vision.

To all the lodges and ranches whose water I photographed. Thank you St. Joe Lodge, Flying B Ranch, and Wapiti Meadow Ranch for allowing me access to places I only dreamed of and for giving me a bed and food while I worked.

To the product sponsors who kept my fishing subjects looking so well provisioned: Sage, Simms, Ex Officio, Mammut, Action Optics, and Thule. Your gear is incredible. Thank you for all the support.

To my wonderful friends at Stoecklein Gallery...thank you Kenton for filling my photo bag with the perfect gear...thank you Kendra for helping me get my film to the right places...thank you Mark for all your scanning expertise...thank you Sarah for such a beautiful layout...and thank you Carrie for all your hard work producing this book.

To all the folks at Silver Creek Outfitters, including Dave J., Dave F., Brian, Jason, and Terry, for answering all my questions. Your passion and knowledge of fly fishing is unparalleled.

To Duffy Witmer and his wonderful family for taking care of me in Santa Barbara while I was in photography school. And a very special thanks to Alyson for introducing me to Dave.

To my good friend Alexander Ellis for allowing me to spook his fish while I taught myself how to take pictures on the river for all those years.

To all the fishermen who let me interrupt their fishing to snap a few photos.

To the Idaho Department of Fish and Game and all the conservation organizations in the state who keep Idaho's rivers in such wonderful condition. Because of their hard work and dedication, Idaho has the best fly fishing in the country.

To the state of Idaho for being unbelievably gorgeous.

And finally, a very special thanks to my mentor David R. Stoecklein. Without his wisdom, time, and patience, I would still be a lost kid with a dream. Dave has taught me the meaning of hard work, brilliant photography, and success. I am forever grateful for his critiques and for the opportunity to work on such a wonderful project.

WWW.RRANDOLPHPHOTOGRAPHY.COM

FOOTNOTES

1. LANDEEN, DAN, STEELHEAD FLY-FISHING IN NEZ PERCE COUNTRY, UNPUBLISHED MANUSCRIPT, P.16, AMATO PUBLICATIONS, PORTLAND, 2006.

2. BLANK, ROBERT H., *INDIVIDUALISM IN IDAHO*, THE TERRITORIAL FOUNDATIONS, P.11, WASHINGTON STATE UNIVERSITY PRESS, PULLMAN, WASHINGTON, 1988.

3. SCHINDLER, HAROLD, *UTAH HISTORY TO GO*, MORMON TRAIL SERIES, THE SALT LAKE TRIBUNE, JULY 8, 1997, QUOTING WILFORD WOODRUFF'S JOURNAL, 3:228-29.

4. ROBST, JULIE LITTS, A WILFORD WOODRUFF DESCENDANT, PERSONAL INTERVIEW REGARDING WORK AND STUDY WITH THE WILFORD WOODRUFF JOURNALS, EMAIL RESPONSE TO KEY IDAHO WORDS THAT MAY SHOW UP IN THE WOODRUFF JOURNALS, DECEMBER 13, 2005.

5. HAMILTON, LADD, *SNOW BOUND*, P. 17, WASHINGTON STATE UNIVERSITY PRESS, 1997.

6. ELIASON, SID, *SNAKE RIVER COUNTRY*, CHARLESTON BOOKS, SALT LAKE CITY, 1987, P. 259 AND STAPLES, BRUCE, *TROUT COUNTRY FLIES*, FRANK AMATO PUBLICATIONS, INC, 2002, PP. 9 AND 108.

7. REED, MARY E. AND KEITH C. PETERSEN, *HARRIMAN FROM RAILROAD RANCH TO STATE PARK*, IDAHO DEPARTMENT OF PARKS AND RECREATION, 1991.

8. HIDY, PETE, *THE FLY FISHER'S WEST*, THE AMERICAN FLY FISHER, JOURNAL OF AMERICAN MUSEUM OF FLY FISHING, VOL.7, NUMBER 2, 1980, P.3.

9. #1 PERSONAL INTERVIEW WITH CLAYNE BAKER, BOISE, IDAHO, DECEMBER 2006. MR. BAKER WROTE THE ARTICLE "THE BIRTH OF THE RENEGADE" FOR SUN VALLEY MAGAZINE.

10. #2 IBID, *SNAKE RIVER COUNTRY*, PP. 213-223.

11. IBID

12. IBID

13. WWW.HENRYSFORK.ORG

14. AMONG THE CONTRIBUTIONS TO THE FLY FISHING LITERATURE THAT TRUEBLOOD MADE ARE *TED TRUEBLOOD'S FISHING HANDBOOK*, FAWCETT PRESS, 1951 AND *THE ANGLER'S HANDBOOK*, THOMAS Y. CROWELL COMPANY, 1949.

15. PERSONAL INTERVIEW WITH LYLE KUNZ, DECEMBER 2006.

16. SWISHER, DOUG AND CARL RICHARDS, *SELECTIVE TROUT*, P. VI CROWN PUBLISHERS, INC., NEW YORK, 1971.

17. KROLL, CHARLES, *SQUARETAIL*, VANTAGE PRESS, 1972, PP. 60-63.

18. PERSONAL INTERVIEW WITH KEITH STONEBRAKER AND BILL NELSON, DECEMBER 2006. ALSO THE READER SHOULD REFERENCE DAN LANDEEN'S BOOK, *STEELHEAD FLY FISHING IN NEZ PERCE COUNTRY*, AMATO PUBLICATIONS, APRIL OF 2006.

19. THE STORY OF THE "BEATS ME" FLY CREATED BY BILL ALSPACH IS TOLD BY KEITH STONEBRAKER AND DAN LANDEEN. BILL CREATED THE FLY TO RESEMBLE AN EMERGING CADDIS, ONE OF THOSE VERY LARGE CADDIS FLIES THAT COME OFF THE CLEARWATER IN THE FALL. THE FLY HAS A PINK ABDOMEN AND A BLACK THORAX WITH A SILVER MYLAR RIB. A WEBBY GRIZZLY HACKLE AND A SQUIRREL TAIL WING COMPLETE THE FLY. BILL HAD GREAT SUCCESS WITH HIS FLY AND WHEN ASKED WHAT HE WAS USING, HE WOULD ALWAYS SAY, "BEATS ME."

20. CLAYNE AND YVONNE BAKER LIVE IN BOISE, IDAHO AND ARE THE OVERSEERS OF THE YOUTH GROUP CALLED THE WOOLLEY BUGGERS. WOOLLYBUGGERBOSS@AOL.COM.

SELF PORTRAIT
RANDY ASHTON

OTHER BOOKS BY STOECKLEIN PUBLISHING

THE WESTERN BUCKLE

THE COWBOY HAT

THE COWBOY BOOT

RANCH STYLE

OUTHOUSES

CATTLE

WESTERN FENCES

CALIFORNIA MISSIONS

SADDLES OF THE WEST

THE AMERICAN QUARTER HORSE

THE HORSE DOCTORS

COWGIRLS IN HEAVEN

THE PERFORMANCE HORSE

LIL' BUCKAROOS

COW DOGS

SPIRIT OF THE WEST

THE AMERICAN PAINT HORSE

THE CALIFORNIA COWBOY

THE IDAHO COWBOY

COWBOY GEAR

THE MONTANA COWBOY

DON'T FENCE ME IN

COWGIRLS

THE TEXAS COWBOYS

THE WESTERN HORSE

SUN VALLEY IMAGES

SUN VALLEY SIGNATURES I, II, III

BIG LOST RANGE
MACKAY, IDAHO